MW00610803

LIVING, LOVING, LETTING GO

Jae —
Thanks for being a
part of the process.
You will continue to
evolve, + make life
better.
Live it. Love it!.

[signature] 22

# Living, Loving, Letting Go

## A Collection of Poems

### RAHMAN JOHNSON

# CONTENTS

Namhar Publishing, LLC
Post Office Box 40213
Jacksonville, FL 32203

ISBN – 9781087885926 (E-Book)
ISBN – 9781087885933 ( E-Book)

First Printing, 2020

# Dedication

To my grandmother Hazel Ross and my mother Ida Ross- Johnson . . .
I love you always.

# Acknowledgments

This collection is dedicated to those who came before. Most importantly those who directly shaped me. My mother and my grandmother are my superstars! These ladies created a confidence in me though believing in possibility and having a passion for change. I could never fully express what it meant to me to be able to provide care for them both in their final years on this side.

For all of the members of Ross, Williams, Berry, Johnson and Aiken Families . . . I am because you are.

For my: extended family of "Auntees" some related and some not but all a part of my growth: Padrica Mendez, Brenda Ross- Towns, Symanthia Stewart, Carrie B. Manor, Carol J. Alexander, Lydia Stewart, Christine A. Murphy, Shirley Thomas, Mary Russ, Bettye Keys- Jackson, Omega Allen, Bettye Woodson, Maguerite Warren, Stephanie Campbell, Justine Redding, JoAnn Williams, Ann Battle, Mary Burke, Adillah Sharrif, Linnie Hilliard- Finley, Corrine Brown, E. Denise Lee, Betty Smith- Holzendorf; Margaret Day- Julian; Cora Reed and Beverly King;

"Uncles": Arthur Johnson, Curtis Stewart, Mansong Kulubally, Imam Umar Sharrif, (my big cousin) Dr. Fredrick D. Harper, Ronnie Belton, Michael Stewart, Dr. Richard Danford, Jr., Ronnie Ferguson, Dr. Howard Dodson, and Marc Little;

My closest friends Gerald Butler, Jason Pearson, Javan Reed, Presiding Elder Elizabeth Yates . . . you are enough! Arlanza Lewis, II – thank you for being the *light* in a tunnel of darkness – the best is yet to come.

My Brothers: Teferri Stewart, William Clemm, Rynara Murphy, Hieden Cummings, Reggie Fullwood, Justin Spiller, James Campbell, Brandon Mack, Jahmal Davis, Raheem Smalls, Frank Cleveland, Nicco Annan, Dewitt Cooper, Richie Danford, Royce Collins, Kenyatta Montgomery, Nova, Bryan C. Daniels, Markell Osler, Wayne Peterson, Damien Lamar, Mikal T. Anderson, Brian "BJ" Johnson Michael Douglas, Kwame Thompson, Emory Snead, Jr., Sensei Vincent Taylor, Dr. Christopher Small and James Washington;

Sisters: Sylvia Perry, Sherry Jackson, Cearrow M. Williams, Tracie Neal Davis,

Cheryl Brown, Ju'Coby Pittman, mjbaker, Alvenia Derban, Dr. Kimberly Davis, Ronline Newell, Marretta Latimer, LaQunta Dixon, Sherre Young, Deidra "Dee-Dee" Sears, Sarah "Peaches" Rollins, Shan Aiken, Ashlie Green and *my sister-friend-auntie mentors* Marcia L. Harris-Daniel and Dr. Ann Wead- Kimbrough;

Those that have passed on: Major Leon Albert "LA" Williams, Jr., Mariano Mendez, Sr., Fred E. "Son Fred" Williams, Jr., Annie Mae Pressley- Allison, Fred "Tommy" Burke, Adewole Okulumele (Anthony Scott), Abu Kareem, Alberta Watkins, Bishop Sadie Gibson and Rev. John Tony Alexander, Bishop Julia Mae Brown. Mother Janie Burke, Jennie Brooks- Aiken, Yvonia "Toni" Donaldson, Evelyn Hooker, Dr. Cynthia Hutchinson- Perry, Shadidi Amma (Stephanie Bryant), Kagiso Goyahkle (Cynthia Hunter) Derrell Allen Jenkins, Bertrand Mayweather, Minnie Louise King, Orian Benjamin Reddick and;

Finally, those life impacting teachers: Pauline Montgomery, Audrey Huskey-Slaughter, Velma Grant, Carolyn Cannon*, Alveria E. Lane. Brenda (Stubbs) Jones, Victoria Neale- Hodge*, Carl Smith*, Brenda Simpkins, Bennie Peeples, Dr. Alphonso Scurry*, Edward Tolliver*, Jewel T. Holloway*, Linda Ghanim*, Marian D. Ellis*, Clifford Buggs, Roslyn Hill- Gullatt, Juanita Tunstall*, Franklin LaVaughan Smith*, Lona Young-Johnson, Ronnie Smith, Doretha T. Haynes- Bodison, Dr. Constance S. Hall, Earlene Toby- Lockett and Coach Charles Lee;

ALL OF MY Learning Teams (students) . . . you make me better!

Quite simply . . . thank you!

# Prologue

My love of poetry and the written word started from childhood. My mother, a Speech-Language Pathologist/Audiologist and my grandmother an educator and administrator, were both lovers of the written word. They passed that love on to me.

I remember borrowing stacks of books from the Haydon Burns Public Library in downtown Jacksonville, Florida. I would take those books home and read until I couldn't read anymore.

At the time, I didn't know that *I* could write.

My Godmother, Rita Perry, was the founder of the Jacksonville Free Press newspaper. Understanding my love for reading she encouraged me to write. For several years, I wrote a weekly column called YouthQuake. Later, I became a writer/reporter and editor for the Florida Times-Union TU Wrap – a teen focused section of the newspaper.

The creative writing spark didn't really hit me until my senior year of High School. My literature teacher, Mrs. Helen D. McAfee required the entire class to write a senior thesis paper and create a Literary Cavalcade. The cavalcade had to include reviews of books, short stories and *poems*. Most importantly, we had to write several poems of our own. Although I didn't consider myself a *writer* (even though I had been journaling since I was 8 years old), that was the moment that started my love of creative writing.

Mrs. McAfee taught us *how* and my African-American studies teacher Coach Charles Lee, taught us the confidence to believe that we could . . . so we did!

Even as I went on to pursue a career in radio, television and news – I never forgot that I was a creator.

Over the years in the privacy of stolen moments, I would write poems on napkins, in journals and on the pages of my heart.

Then in 2019, my mother passed away.

That moment sparked a release to share my work with the world.

During my life, I heard a quote that was attributed to Buddha . . . or so I thought. I had always considered the quote to be profound.

As I started to think about the quote even deeper, I looked it up. I found out the actual quote didn't come from Buddha but actually from Jack Kornfield's, Little Buddha Instruction Book.

> *"In the end these things matter most: How well did you love? How fully did*
> *you live? How deeply did you let go?"*

Living, Loving Letting Go, is compiled through the prism of these three major movements in the journey of life. I hope you enjoy the journey as I share moments that have shaped and continue to shape my life.

In the words of one of my favorite writers Audre Lorde, from her poem For Each of You, *"love as deeply as if it were forever . . . knowing nothing lasts eternal"*.

Here's to experiencing the fullness and freedom of eternal love.

# 1

# On Living

Each day we rise, is another opportunity to learn the lessons.

This journey has taught me that there is no such thing as failure. There are only lessons to learn! One thing I know for sure is that each day is another opportunity to learn.

I met a guru of life on my journey. His name was Bernard V. Gregory. He was one of the wisest people I knew.

He once said, "Life is God's gift to you. What you do with that life is your gift back to God. If I were you, I'd choose to give God my best".

That is why I choose to live fearlessly.
As we live, we learn.
As we learn, we grow.
As we grow, we teach.
As we teach, we evolve!

Such is the way of life or life as it should be.

~ 1 ~

poem

your lips glide over me like the finest silk draped over a polished
marble pillar
you create in me the unexpected when you add your nuances to
my substance

i am zydeco music at a party on the bayou in louisiana i
am a batá sounding the rhythm of the orisha in cuba i am
the pulse in hip-hop; bronx, new york, circa 1983
i am the tongues spoken by grandma at the small wooden church in
augusta

i am the haunting voice of the high priestess, foreboding, yet
beautiful nonetheless
reminding us to be  us
i am all of these things and more when you possess my essence

when i was created, even during my evolution,
i thought i would be destined to stay here being exactly who i
was,
doing exactly what i did and just waiting
right here waiting, for who knew what.

your breath of life made my existence manifest and i tell the
story.

i am the grief in mammy's heart as her child is ripped away from
her bosom

i am the gaze of the new puppy as he looks at little boy -- his new
master

i am the clack of the thunder and the flash in the lightning as
you hide under your covers (fear me)
i am the soft smile of the ancestor, no words, who is closer than she
knows to transition

i am the gentle tingle of loves first kiss.

i am – your poem.

# I LEAD TO SERVE

*for Mother Elizabeth Ann Seton and Seton Hall*

I lead to serve and serve to lead, seeking a future that will be,
challenged to change a destiny.

Nuanced precepts of the life I live, means
there is something more to give The Hall
taught me to work in love.
To lead to serve to be above.
To judge *not* those who may not have,
For those who do, reminding them of the path.

The path of responsibility, to be more, to do more – to ACT!

I lead to serve and serve to lead
It's my charge to keep on the road I seek.

A saint among women, we carry her name
She showed us the path by leading the way
As the roads get tough, oft they will do,
she relied on a scripture tried and true

*"The Lord IS my shepherd. I shall not want"*

I lead to serve and serve to lead, a link in the chain of destiny.
Changing the world with simple acts,
enlightening the masses with truth and facts
Forging uncharted ways, changing life today
Knowing the when's and how's and why's,
seeing the future through brand new eyes.

Leading to serve, I serve to lead
Answering the charge, the Hall had for me.

# THE PATH

The paths that we choose in the labyrinth of life makes our volatile unions all the more unique.

Certainly, I see beyond the thicket and yearn for the promises of the foreboding aspect.
To gain admission to clarity, universal existential thought must be sacrificed

I wondered at the crossroads who could navigate the way
I wondered if the one presupposed was just a figment of mythic reality
I wondered if proportion or lack thereof provided fuel for my quandary

Dazed and confused like the multitude of zombies that inhabit our plane
I found myself moving further and further away to a place that I had never reached before
. . . . CONFUSION

Once I understood that understanding was the confession of ignorance and the fact that I knew what I did not know, made me wise . . . I knew that I was on the PATH!

## WE WERE THERE
*(after the 2006 Bill Duke Actor's Boot Camp at the ABFF)*


Spending time by oceans shore
We were there
Coming from far and near
We were there
Open like sponges, ready for the knowledge we would receive . . .
.
We were there


Barely inside the new millennium at a time when all had returned
to soul
The universe cried for artists, to bring joy and tell stories and
pass along traditions
There was technique to the work of the artists and so we had to
learn
Most importantly we had to learn – to forget all that we've
learned
Described like walking into nothingness and falling back with
no fear
Like reliance on faith
Faith in HIM, faith in ourselves, faith in the process

We were there.


Spending time by ocean's shore

We were there Coming from far and near

We were there

Open like sponges, ready for the knowledge we would receive...

We were there


A King of a man, a guide sent from on high . . . was there

He, like a high priest of the art

Teaching the traditions of old, inspiring the creation of new,
Taking impossible nothingness and creating possibility

HE had paved the way for us to walk and now was showing us

the path.

Finally, we would be able to silence the cries of the universe and
make her laugh!


We were there – allowing them to come down

There in the place where some of the great masters had been
There in the place where at one-time we could perform but not

sleep or eat,

Preparing for greatness – we were there!


Invoking those gone before, I saw

Dorothy Dandridge

Sammy Davis, Jr.

Stepin Fetchit

Hattie McDaniels

Woody Strode

Esther Rolle

Paul Robeson

They were there!!

At the place where he transitioned, even Ossie Davis was there –
they were all there!

Sooner than later we will tell the stories and share the anecdotes
of the time when we were there

Sooner than later giving credit in thankfulness to God for

sending us a griot of the work.


Spending time by oceans shore

We were there Coming from far and near

We were there

Open like sponges, ready for the knowledge we would receive...

I remember . . . we were there.

~ 5 ~

## EXPERIENCE

I wonder if the experience of being over experienced is a unique experience.

Will those experiences allow my masterpiece to blossom?
I won't allow the resolution of a predicated existence to propel me

I move only through locomotion that edifies my soul
I move upon paths that have yet to be discovered by the Multitude

As my experience deepens, the panic lessens then intensifies, then mellows
The depth of this experience makes the pool of knowledge widen
                    – and I yearn to learn
                              . . . and experience

# THE CHAKRA

The Chakra vibrate within my soul and I am released
As the energy spins in a continuum of knowledge, the
things I *thought* I knew were illuminated as lies.
The energy of my inner power
revealed the passion of my purpose.
I succumbed to *this* passion – true passion!
Passion that I had never known before.

I, not yet ready for what was in store
Not ready for the power of the chakra
The strength of my chakra knew no definition
Naked I stood as my chakra allowed me to see
[Things with my third eye]
Things as they should rightly be
Unleashing the energy of the chakra
Taming the power of the – kah –
I was uninhibited!
Still not yet ready for what was in store
The power of the chakra gave me more
The strength of the chakra, a center of power, even now refuses to
be defined.

The Chakra

# About Happy 2 B Nappy

In 2001, my twin (we have the same birthday), Sherry, took her talents to the next level and opened a natural hair salon.

She was my mother's loctician and mine too.

My friend did a thing.
She do hair.
I do words.

Here is what I did.

# HAPPY 2 B NAPPY

I'm Happy 2B Nappy,
Happy Being in the skin that I'm in.
No matter what they say or feel – no choice but to kneel Entering the door once more,
I feel the vibe engulf my body, and I know there is more in store.
Staring into the abyss, moving like a spinning top
I stopped combing my mind so my thoughts would lock.
The lady standing behind me grooms my locked thoughts

In her grooming process it was knowledge that she dropped.
A place where I can escape,
Be me.
Be free.
Believe.
In me . . .
I learn these things Happily nappy!
Small corner in historic hood, the best place to be.

I'm so happy being nappy.
Happy Being in the Skin That I'm In!

# TRUTH

I am a bright and full moon shining on a dark and cloudless
night,
Brighter than the north star and cooler than polar ice caps, I am.
Leading the charge of change through exploration . . .
     . . . . of myself
     . . . . of humanity
     . . . . of higher consciousness . . . I am.

Cavernous craters of knowledge await my discovery.
Even in the fullness of Kronos, I could not digest the secrets I see.
Long ago I released loneliness when I realized that I was

connected to the world.

The thin sliver of thread that connects us all,
is stronger than tungsten and more intricate than the most
unique tapestry on the Fates loom.
The connection, though invisible makes some question its
tangibility and balk at its existence.
There is no replacement for TRUTH and placebo is revealed al-
ways as an impostor.

## UNTITLED –
### *Life Thoughts and Stuff, I Guess*

Life is a riddle.

I mean it's not like this is something new.

There are things that happen in the experience of life that aren't supposed to be explained.

So why bother?

The questions are infinite.

Then again so are the answers.

Just not at the same time.

Why do people do the things they do?

Why do we act the way we do?

How come?

I suppose the simple explanation is that nothing can really be explained.

Confusing.

The more I learn that life's twists and turns are unavoidable, the more comfortable that makes me with myself.

# About Oma

Grandma-hood is hard! Or so I hear.

My friend was really close to being and grandmother and wasn't quite old enough or ready enough to use the term grandma, or grandmother.

Plus, she came from a long line of divas (Ms. Anna-Frances [ her mama] was something special)!

So, she settled in nn the German word for Granny . . . simply OMA!

## OMA

Seeing the scene of time with eyes of wisdom,
My focused future places me squarely NOW!
Releasing the bonds of culture,
Finally free . . . .
I AM ME!
My womb has held greatness, which begat greatness.
My strength, ever present as the tradition is carried on.

I – walking on water
I – moving mountains
I – creating possibility out of the impossible.
I am the universe's perfect expression of this moment.

Beyond sight, at the edge of night
Morning glows between my toes -- I am OMA!
Lavender lenses of gentle wisdom shade my view and here
I sit . . . Knowing and being ME!

## MANIFEST

Our meeting yesterday was like a millennial occurrence –
monumental.
I said,
You said,
We saw,
They did,
And there we were. . . .
In circumstances of our own development
Evolution was inevitable
Timing however was questionable, and
the burning of learning remained.
My enigma was a treasure that others could only hope to fathom
Yet you looked effortlessly at the secrets I thought I held
and smiled.
Waiting for the time when you would say simply, "I already
knew".

A connection was made.
Thicker than blood,
Deeper than shared experiences,
Larger than life.

The unspoken, unbroken bond was there but faith and trust could
only come
with testing the strength of the invisible bridge to nowhere.

Your eyes are fierce and piercing yet gentle
Your mind, sharp and quick yet palatable
Your actions, confident and decisive yet vulnerable
Your speech, resonant yet alluring
Carrying the weight of the world with ease
You are an expression of this moment's perfection

The moments that continue to unfold as if by magic,
finds you in creation of an even better self.
In this moment, I am honored to know perfection in the person that
is you.

One who enjoys and accepts,
Comprehends and interprets,
Speaking softly but powerfully.
The best life has to offer is contained within you
The millennial moment meeting that created a kinship of self-
expression is now manifest
And the lessons continue

## ~ 12 ~

## TRUTH OF THE SUN

Ready, Set, GO . . .
Here I Come
Come I with the Knowledge of the Sun
Cranial Abnormalities
Make the formality of finality
None less than a malady
Soliel de soir
I see not and it sees not me
Blind eye closed
Mind opened to the three-sixty degree
Heat rises
Mind violence
Turned over in contemplation
Further though speculation
I give verbal ejaculation
Which should inspire adulation
Not to mention relaxation
Now I'm set to go
Go to places anointed unreachable
I authored the prequel, the book and the sequel

Yet you ask me how I am set to go?
Set thought the power of the sun

I stare into you with righteous rays

Destroying retinas and corneas if you have no
shades

Only shade of purity can shield you from these
rays
Today, no play.
Your conscience will sway from the heat of these rays
Ase!
Sun Set, end of day . . .

# About Life Words

Over the years . . . I have written poems for family and friends as they celebrated major milestones. This was a BIG birthday for Uncle Mariano.

Although I was traveling and couldn't be there in person, I sent a poem. It was about the story of a little boy and his Cuban father sharing a moment.

**Mariano Pedro and Padrica Mendez**

Little did I know, that birthday would be his last. I was glad that I was able to celebrate him while he lived.

## ~ 13 ~

## LIFE WORDS

*for the Birthday Celebration of Mariano Mendez, Sr.*

The Father said to the Son . . .

"My child, what I want most in the world is to give you my knowledge and experience. But what value would a man my age have, if a child your age could have my experience?

And what value would your childhood have if you had my experience from the start?"

Those wise words being spoken from father to son,
They stayed in the boy's heart his heart, as he
journeyed the path.
Second child, first boy full of the spark of life.
He was ready to learn and grow and work.
Boy became man.
Man became leader.
Leader became teacher . . . and so he did his work.
He'd become more than his dreams could hold.
Striving and being and growing and seeing,
he followed father's words and remade the mold – in *his* image.

There were journeys to foreign lands and war and more work,
But the words of the father remained.
Learn and grow and experience the experience, he recalled.

He created family,
exemplified light and always had a laugh and a smile.
There to be, there to see,
lending a hand for all in need

His sewing sowed seeds of lineage.
His weaving explored the loom of life.
Yet he, simple as could be, knew that as he lived and grew
His father's words were true.

When the time came . . .
he shared those same words to his son and his son's son
Those focused and powerful -- words of life!

## THE WALKING MAN

The walking man,
Feeble and bent from years of age,
looked insignificant as he crossed the street for his dinner.

A two piece no pepper from Church's.

His significance was more than they could fathom, for he *was*
knowledge.
I could only imagine the secrets that he kept locked in the vault of
his brain
Secrets in youth we try desperately to attain
Knowledge through growth we could only hope
to gain
For or our paces were too hectic
Running here and going there
Doing this and trying that
Not taking the time as tradition said,
To gain the knowledge from the elder head
No not us
Not atall.

When our elders become elder
We think them feeble and weak and unable to go the distance,

We place them in the back.

In the back of our minds,

In the back of our lives,
Forgetting, that if we were wise, we would know:

> *that the young man is chosen because of his strength*
> *and the elder because he knows the way.*

Old man's insignificance
Then becomes insignificant,
to those who have no significance.

I attributed this dissension to the lack of intervention of the
generation that came before.
Yet we wonder why things are so hard
And we wonder why at times we aren't smart
But we really shouldn't wonder
Because the map we should be using, we neglect
And allow the elders to take their knowledge to the grave

The walking man or the sitting lady
Old and feeble with age
Possess the keys to secrets eternal
That we're forever trying to reach

I was there when the walking man feeble and bent from years of
age
Crossed the street for his dinner
As I watched him walk and falter
I felt conviction in his steps
Fire still in his eyes
I knew of his importance
I thirsted for his knowledge

He ordered, a two piece no pepper.

I paid.

It was the least I could do to buy his dinner.
The Walking Man.

# About Adieu

Turning 30 was a moment.

Really, it was the realization of my mortality.

It's not as if I didn't know it before but as I reflected . . . life became REAL.

This was the moment that I said good-bye to my 20's.

Like I said, it was a moment.

## 15

## ADIEU

I bid you adieu.

Goodbye, I say as I see you leave, never to return again.
I can remember it as if it were yesterday when I met you.
It felt as though it took me ages to get there but you were
waiting on me.

A new rhyme, a stitch in time – you were waiting on me.
I embraced you when you arrived,
I jumped in your arms, I was ready for the ride.
Not knowing what was in store or where this road would lead
I thought I was ready for you and you had things to show me
Putting mouth on foot and foot in mouth,
you taught me how to straighten the whole thing out.

When I met you, I knew it all – it was clear to me
From 0 to 1 then two and three.
The more you stayed with me – the more I grew, the deeper I be-
came, the more I knew.
I was beginning to yearn and you were showing me that this was
only the beginning.

Blind faith held me and your few years gave me strength.
Running races with no feet, eating food with no meat.
You allowed my evolution, and that created greatness.

I thought it was me – yet the God in me kept me from being weary
and he allowed me to see you.

For many, my rising action would have been a climax but mine
was yet to come
Still I rise – In search of . . .

Nevertheless, as I entered the center of the time I'd know you
Blinders fell off and soon our relationship would  be
through
Mind's eye now open, as if from a baby's first sight
Blinking and wondering, why can't I see the light.

I was a new creature, a new being riding your wings to destiny
It was a turning and nurturing point in our relationship,

I was loving you and you were loving me,
yet leaving oh too quickly.

I ran the race and with reality I was faced.
The lesson was mine to learn and with humility and
understanding it finally made sense:

*When you run a race, the lesson is sometimes in the running and*
*not in the winning –*

Now I understood.
My mind was open
My life was ready

The knowledge that I thought I possessed meant nothing

For infinite wisdom was unattainable.

*So, I could swim unabashedly in knowledge and still not know an inkling of what there was to know.*

All of a sudden, I knew it was my calling to facilitate knowledge and inspire thought
Had found the platform and was ready for the next path – but you had other plans for me

I was snatched up.
The platform I had planned was no more

My platform became the world
I was at the place I had envisioned.

It was no mirage, the truth you bring
All eyes on me – must be righteous with this thing

I was so busy and preoccupied doing what I do,
I was helping others but sooner than later, there would be no more you.

Your time with me was dwindling but silently you held me, you cradled me and made me forget that you would one day be gone.

Along the path, I saw my ancestor's journey to another plane
Along the path, I followed my destiny and longed for family
Along the path, I almost traveled the path eternal
Along the path, I finally discovered that **GOD** had been with *me* the entire time.

So now, as I take the cue that we will part,
I think of you in gladness and melancholy.
Fondly, I'll remember our time.

You made me laugh, you made me cry – you made me fine!

I bid you Adieu.

It is the respect and admiration that I earned though you
I am evolving
I am learning
I am loving
I am being
I am giving
I am feeling
I am the me that I am
I am the me that I will become
I am....... because I experienced you.

Truly, I know I shall never see you again but you served your
purpose
You did your time,
YOU opened my mind to possibility.

So as you turn to leave,
Sadly, fondly, yet proudly,
I bid you adieu.

# Loving

# On Loving

The Ancient Greeks had eight ways of knowing and defining love.

They were:

Eros – Erotic Love

Philia – Affectionate Love

Ludus – A playful love

Pragma – Longstanding Love

Philautia – Self-Love

Xenia – Hospitality or love of guests

Agape – Unrequited selfless love

Storge – The love of parents toward children; Familial Love

Although love at its core-essence is undefinable, categorizing love is in many ways helpful to understanding love.

I am all about expanding the horizon of possibilities.

Yet the question exists, will we ever really know what love is? Really?

Even deeper, I believe — that the answer to this question today, will usually not be our reality tomorrow.

When it comes to love of any kind, there has to be synergy.

A caring friendship (agape or philia) is foundationally far more important before jumping off into some kind of eros type relationship. That way, if some- thing ever happens to any other part of the relationship the connection re- mains. That's true for all facets of love.

When I'm dating, one of the first questions I ask is, "Were you in love with the person in your last relationship"?

Then the follow up is, "Do you still love that person"? The answers are where it gets interesting.

If I hear, "I was in love *then,* but I don't love him anymore", it sends up a red flag.

What I know for sure, is that love is an emotion that doesn't end with the demise of an erotic relationship.

If you once love someone truly, you will love them forever.

Does this mean that you'll be in love forever? Hell no!

I didn't say be *in* love, but the essence of love will always be there.

Regardless of *how* you love, *that* you love is what's most important.

## 16

# I CALL THEM FORTH

*a poem for the two who became one*


I call them forth

From yesteryear and over there, I call them forth
The nameless ones, the blameless ones, I call them forth

The leaders, the seekers, creators the BE-ers . . . I call them forth
With drum rhythms of circadian synchronicity,
we call them forth to share the moment
The two come as one and one
Yet they stand as 10,000

They the ones who spoke to deities
with unpronounceable names
They the ones who crossed and thrived
They the ones who cleared the landscape with their blood,
laid the foundation with their words
and built monuments of their sojourn with their bones
They the ones who survived . . .

In silence.

We welcome their essence from far and near
We sit in their presence we call them here to hallowed ground –
because we said so.

Alafia, Akwaba, Kunjani, Jambo, Indemin Walatschu, Salaam

In every way, in every place we celebrate because of YOU!

At times this unrequited love, was an indicted love
This unsanctioned love was still sent from above
and that made it right.
This unbelievable love,
this unretractable love,
this irreplaceable love –
is the liberation of life!

Our celebration embraces, your presence and the pith of your
existence.
It all leads to now.

In our tongue we speak gratitude.
Thanking you for celebrating our blessing with your presence.
Your work here continues as you return to the beyond.

We rest well embracing your teaching and your BE-ing
knowing that we
CALLED THEM FORTH
                    . . . AND THEY CAME!

## 17

## ODE TO LOVE

That moment I held you and looked beyond the surface -that was love.
We tried and said no, then life said yes and it was what it was . . .
It was love.

And for just a moment, I was touched by emotion that made motion easy for me
I was believing what my eyes could not see
In just that moment, love had found me.

Found me wandering aimlessly in an abyss of bottled emotion
Like a nomad wandering through the desert looking for an oasis that would quench my thirst
Then came you ...
You couldn't have been a lie
I saw you standing there too good to be true
Good for me, even better for you
We met by happenstance, CIRCUM-CHANCE most importantly we met
I took that to be a sign,
that your future was mine and you'd
Be there right by my side

Things you talked about settled easily on my mind, and if I
needed to talk – you'd be right on time I was loving you and
feeling you and longing for you everyday but like the end of most
good things, I got in the way

Couldn't top the love
Didn't want to stop the love
Wasn't careful 'bout to drop the love, trying not to let the  love
go
You were nothing I could have imagined - exceeding my wildest
dreams,
My heart was ripping at the seams - for you
Now the other side of me felt like I was in a fix,
Bound up and wrapped up and tied up in this
I felt like I was shackled and gagged and cuffed and put in a box
locked up and stopped up and pinned up - just blocked

You were there for me when the hard times got rough
You were there for me when I'd just had enough
You were there - can't deny it you were there
And then there was me
Although committed to you saying the words made me weary
I couldn't and you wouldn't and what should have been ain't
And if tomorrow were yesterday, I'd have told you I'd wait.
Now that I'm older and stronger and wiser, you can't be found
and my heart's like a miser's
I've locked up my heart and thrown away the key, I suppose no one
is ready for the real me.
Except you ...
I don't ever think I could love like that again
So if you hear me,

And you feel me
And you know her.
Tell her I miss her.
Tell her I need her ~ tell her,
I can finally say it
I LOVE YOU.

MY ODE TO LOVE.

# ANSWER ME

It's been 24 Hours since I've heard your voice.
That pains me.
It's only been 7 days and I'm already counting the ways I
think of you.
Quickly I'm smelling love in the most inopportune places.
Sensing you love me too but this was too much.
I am a full vessel and your cup runneth over.
Your deafening distance tickled my awareness.
Knowing me wanting you.
Knowing you wanting me.
We Supernova.
Bound by the vow of promised friendship,
we smile through the pain.
Love and Animosity
Attraction and Resentment
You are here ........yet you are not.
A longing to be with the one we see reflected in the mirror
but not quite ready for the responsibility.
I'm calling.
I'm trying.
I'm reaching.
Answer me, please.
Please.
Answer me.

## BED-STUY

You are not beyond reach.

In fact, you are right there.

Yet the unspoken words of infatuation and feelings remain . . . . unspoken.

I wonder as I wander, what it would be like to wake up to you in the morning.
The bliss of a first kiss; no words – just knowing – just being – THERE!

The is-ness of we-ness is supreme.

We speak often.

When I hear your voice, I wonder as I wander, if you feel the same attraction I do.
Then I think. I know you do!
I don't know -------- but I know.

Neither is willing to make a move but when the time is right – the time will be right.

Your unshakeable confidence makes me smile at the circum-stance.

I am aware that I don't know you and yet, I just may love you.

Nestled away in a corner.
Being you.

In Bed-Stuy.

# FEELING HIM

Feeling him, yes, I'm feeling him
In ways I've never felt before
People not understanding the way I feel,
Or the way he feels – not sexual just real
So I'm feeling him
Continuously feeling him
The way I feel again, is not revealed in sin

And I wonder why I am feeling him like that
Am I the son of sheclack-clack?
Does it just exist in my mind that I feel him like that?
I feel him in ways that before I couldn't imagine and now
Cannot comprehend
Cannot fathom
Cannot understand
Yet, I'm still Feeling Him . . .

## FINGERS AND TOES

I miss you.
I can count the days, I've known you on fingers and toes

Yet for you and I, the intensity was much too much to bear
You had him and I had . . . me . . . just me
And in this moment we had what shouldn't be
But it existed

Just the day before, we held.
Not able to get enough of each
other.
Gazing deeply into our souls we touched, "that" place.

Today you look away.
Not in disgust, trying to forget the magic of lying in my arms.
What wasn't supposed to be – felt like it should have been.
There I was again shining like the sun – being my best me – just
me.
And still it's way too much.

Young love remembered and yet can't form the words to say it's
love at all.
Eyes tell the story that has been searching for a voice.
Emotion tumbles forth and we are not ready.

Smiling a faint smile that hurts to form.

You are me.

You know me.

Even though I can count the days I've known you on fingers and toes.

## HOME - A HAIKU

My light of love shines brightly
Missing you madly
You the home I call my home

# ~ 23 ~

## I LOVE YOU, I THINK

I mean, I love you . . .
I think
I think that right now you caught me just at that time
at the time when I was repairing the damage
to the wall around my heart
though others tried to chip away at the steely exterior
you were the benefactor of their work.
I told myself from the beginning that it was, what it was . . . simply
that which it was
you were more than that
you the product of imagination and fantasy
manifested on me . . . and I did not need this now

Nevertheless, I love you . . . I think

# NEXT TO ME

*(In Houston)*

You sat next to me at dinner by sheer happenstance

I smiled a pleasant smile, not knowing that you sitting next to me
was predestined, and right where I needed to be.

Gently, I placed my hand on your thigh and you exhaled
Comfortably . . . right next to me!

I think one day . . . . maybe you'll say, "I enjoy him waking up
next to me"!

My reaction to your passion cemented our interaction

In that moment there was traction... all for the one sitting next
to me.

# RUNNING THROUGH MY THOUGHTS

*2.13.11 A Vintage Miles Day -- 10:54 am*

I see you there in my imagination,
running quickly and hiding in my thoughts, like I can't see you.

In time you will be fine with letting me love you
the way that you deserve.

Our existence is like ripened fruit on the vine,
ready to fall at any moment into an abyss of bliss!

I see you there.
So keep running.
I'll wait here for you to notice me.
Watching and waiting.

You the one running and hiding in my thoughts.

## WIND

I didn't request your presence but you arrived, nevertheless.
Like a wind from the south
You made it your business to blow in my direction.
Insurrection.
Introspection.
Frequent Interjections.
My mind lacked the consistency to gain some direction and I
found myself hurdling toward . . .
YOU

# YOU SEEM FAMILIAR TO ME

As I think about it.........when I met you
You seemed familiar to me

Like a fetus sharing that close dark space
that allowed us to evolve,
Nothing I thought I wanted but everything I needed.
Your energy was alluring
because in its simplicity was familiarity . . .
And the familiar was beautiful

A cacophoning sound of funk on page
Every Good Boy Does Fine
Sharps and flats accentuate the experience
You came to my F-A-C-E
And allowed me just to be
To make my music through a symphony that was your soul.

In the essence of all that is, you seem familiar to me
Looking into your eyes, more reflective that peering into a
mirror
Transports me deeper within myself

This Supreme Love deeper than love itself had yet to be defined
Which is why moments after I met you I knew . . . oh I knew!
I pushed you away as not to play the game.

In time that push attracted me more to the me that was in you
because I was comfortable with the familiar

You see I had been in love before,
Been in like in a past life
Even been in comfort once or twice.
But now that I've grown, I'm older and wiser
Time reveals all and I see the fire – the burn and yearn of love
that IS

So comfortable as good as can be
Just really won't do for someone like me.
I'm craving the me that can't be that I see in YOU.

You . . . you, seem familiar to me

If you can't right now, I'll wait patiently
In that familiar place a beautiful space
Just you and me AND me!

## 28

## THE FIRST DAY OF THE REST OF
## YOUR LIFE

*For: Ajile Ogunsegun (Ida Ross-*
*Johnson) A Celebration of Life*

I never understood what the bond was Just
knew it was there.
Never quite knew the words to express how I feel about you,
Just knew they were there.

From the labor pains,
To protecting the young from the rain and sheltering from the
storm those who were lost,
You are mother of generations,
Celebrating the essence of life's continuation
Though helping the life of another.

Words to describe you have yet to be invented,
For your love has yet to reach a boundary.
There to support when I had,
There to supply when I had not.
You realize, summarize, chastise and proselytize, even baptize

With your knowledge and your love all who come in your presence.

Privileged to know you I am, for my relation to you bestows royalty on me.

Always wise beyond your years you were blessed
when God made you,
He took from Mary Magdalene, Faithful Sarah, Queen Nandi and even MARY
When he made you, he knew what we knew not
When he made you he knew a masterpiece was begot.

So we,
Celebrate your existence with a prayer and a shout!
Celebrate your existence with thanksgiving!
Celebrate your existence knowing that now you have further earned the right to walk in greatness!

This is the first day of the rest of your life.
Now queen mother, take advantage of your destiny!

## 29

# LOVING BLACKNESS

*(One Morning)*

One morning I woke up and discovered that I was black
Now it's not as if I had wondered before
But this particular morning I was convicted and convinced to
atone my roots, to rediscover the fact that I was black

I was black like the tribal drums of yesteryear
Boom ta ta boom ta ta boom –
This connection to my blackness gave me
understanding of their mysterious language.
The talk of the drum -- a confirmation of my blackness.

I was black like songs of the songs of the ancestors,
sang to powerful deities controlling the universe
Obatalata weni sede ude oba laea fed e le
I understand the songs,
I could feel the chants to Chango, Yemonja and Osun –
Thanked Esu for leaving me be
The music of the ancestors, a confirmation of my blackness

I be black like the chastised poetry of Phyllis Wheatley.
Couldn't say what she really wanted to say,
Cause missus wouldn't teach her all the things in this new
tongue
So she say what they wanted to hear:

*T'was mercy brought me from my Pagan land, Taught my
benighted soul to understand Some view our sable race with
scornful eye,*

*"Their colour is a diabolic die." Remember, Christians,
Negroes, black as Cain,*

*May be refine'd, and join th' angelic train.*

The chastity of Wheatley -- a confirmation of my blackness. I

be black like silence . . .
The silence my family endured though the middle passage
Huddled in the bosom of JESUS – awaiting who knew what
The silence of suffering – a confirmation of my blackness.

I be black like negro spirituals sang by a mammy who'd just had
enough
Sang with the tenacity of a barracuda
Swing low sweet chariot,
Com-min' for to carry me home
A testament of my blackness, still.

I be black like, like blues songs that told of the pain
and promises of the future
I be sad from the blues but happy from the music Like
when Muddy say:
"Got my mojo working but it just don't work on you" (I

love you woman)

Still my blackness.

I be black like the speeches of Jordan and King and Jesse,
Black like the action of Garvey.
Black like the conviction of Chisholm.
Black like the boldness of Tavis and the confidence of Angela Davis
and RYE!
Man I be black and all that is me

Black like the jokes of Pryor and Murphy
Black like the talk of Robin Harris, when he says:
"Woman goes into a store and says to the saleslady – I'd like to
see a dress that fits me .
Saleslady says, I'd like to see a dress that fits you too"
I be black like laughter -- that too is my blackness.

I be black like Neo-Soul
Jill Scott, DeAngelo and Erykah Badu with the Roots in tow,
Talking about where is Res and where is Emperor Prince
And in comes Prince hand in hand with N'Dambi followed by
Lucy Pearl *(and who knows who's in that group but they still* JAM)
I be black like – and if you don't want to be down with me,
then you don't want to be from my Apple Tree . . .

That's all me . . .
I be black beyond belief
Black Beyond Comprehension

I am your negro
I am your nigger
I am your kaffir
I am your colored
I am your African-American
I'll be your boy

and in some cases when you catch me wrong – sap suckin' so and
so

But I'm still bad and black with a pot belly and a skin tight shirt
(*'casue you know we will*)
Or a six pack and baggy jeans .

Bad – cause I'll take a butt whipping like Tyson and still keep
talking stuff
Bad – playing tennis like Venus and Sirena – so what you sick of
us – we WILL win again
Bad – like LeRoy Butler – running and jumping and playing and
taggin'

One morning I woke up and discovered I was black.
Still learning what it means – but happy to be ME!

# ~ 30 ~

## SOMETIMES

On the way headed to reality to break if off and earn my freedom
I took a detour
And for just a moment, I experienced fantasy.
A fanatical fantastic foie gras of epic proportions - - - was there!
I standing at the threshold of breaking yet another heart – my
own -- stopped trying to do it for myself and placed my order with
the universe
Moving out of her way, I let her do her thing.
Supreme thought.
Higher Consciousness.
Belief.
It was all manifest!
All that I imagined was there.
Everything I thought was brought.
It excited me to know,
That sometimes, Dreams really do come true . . . .
And the ONE, sometimes really does come through . . . .
Sometimes.

# Letting Go

# On Letting Go

I guess in this process – life that is . . . I finally get it!

You already know what's true in this moment could quickly change in the next.

The lesson however is still important, so here goes.

Anything I have is ephemeral. So why even try to hold on to it.

I read the work of Eckhart Tolle and learned that the
three modalities of awakened doing are acceptance,
enjoyment and enthusiasm.

Whatever the thing is, regardless of the circumstances – don't judge it.

Just BE.

Experience the moment. Learn the lessons.

If you can first accept the thing . . . then you might enjoy it.

If you enjoy it, you may be enthused by it
and enthusiasm changes the energy of your existence!

In all that we do, letting go is honestly the hardest part.

There are people who think love is harder when you have to let go.
I suppose it is.

In essence, the hardest thing to do is just to let go and know
that the experience was exactly what you needed when you needed it.

Whether it's love, death or simply transition -- the importance of letting go is
quite simply elevation!

## 31

## IF I KNEW I DIDN'T HAVE MUCH TIME

If I knew I didn't have much time,
I'd have found a brighter way to shine
A more exclusive way to be
So that you'd be proud of me . . .

If I knew I didn't have much time
If I'd have known it'd be so quick, I'd have never gotten sick
So only smiles would light our way
As we enjoyed both night and day

If I knew I didn't have much time
If I'd have thought you'd leave this space, taking all your style
and grace
I'd have tried to learn even more
Before you entered heaven's door
If I knew I didn't have much time

However, what I knew not made me wise
For my bliss it made me blind . . . to the possibility of today

So I loved you fiercely evermore,

I believe I brought honor to your door.
I treasured each moment of dark and light
I learned from your tenacity, your strength, your might.

Yes the time was short but I'd do it all the same
For what some see as loss for me is glorious gain
The grand love you had for me here
Is greater and boundless over there
So no . . . we didn't have much time
That time I'll cherish, yours and mine

And now I see it was just enough time . . . Simply DIVINE!

## 32

# BEAH!

*for*
*Emmy Award Winning Actor, Activist, Teacher and Philosopher*
*Beah Richards*

Lisa Gay Hamilton, made sure that that the black woman speaks…still.
Thank you.

On the screen I saw her dignity
The stage revealed her grace . . .
I knew not how she touched me but Lisa brought it home
She didn't allow constrictions to her life or her existence
She had to BEAH!

From Mississippi to the height of L.A., she reigned supreme
Teaching her art, preaching her art,
Living her art BEAHing who she was.

She said, "I'll never apologize for BEAHing me"!
Awards she was happy to receive but more than that
Her reward was living life.

Teaching others and at the time the struggle,

And because she took no nonsense her trials were doubled

But she had to BEAH . . . the BEAH that she should.
She had to share her love, she promised she would

She was more than ordinary
Living contrary to the beliefs
Wide nose, dark skin, kinky hair – she
had unapologetic African beauty
To meet her was a treat
And the path, she was always ready to teach.

It was easy for her because all she had to do was BEAH

The Black Woman Spoke

## 33

## SEEDS OF LIGHT

The universe knew that *she* would create *her* before the dawn of time.

She knew in this space, in that place – that she would be a force!

A fierce lioness protector.
A gentle solace in the torrent.
A well of light.

Yesteryear's expression and the vision of tomorrow
were the points on her compass
She knew her work was to sow seeds that
would yield harvests of knowledge
that she wouldn't witness . . . yet her work continued.

In dignity.
Through strife.
With love.

She was the one that the universe was needed at that time.
Her love was transformational.
Her work did not end with her transition.

Ever growing,

Ever nurturing,

Ever evolving,
Ever sowing, her seeds of light.

## 34

# HE LIVED

*(a poem for Roy, Jr.)*

He lived!

The man lived and inspired us to be our best and do our best and to embrace the world.
He lived boldly and emphatically but most importantly -- he lived authentically.

The poetry and verse of his life,
was the rhythm and rhyme of strife -- and love.
Each moment was an incandescent reflection of
nuanced perfection that captured the moment.

To know him, was to love him
To love him, was to embrace him
To embrace him was to touch the essence of a star!

Like a Grand Duke of words he spoke to crowds
and classrooms through simple speak with complex elegance.

The man . . . he lived!
His style, impeccable.

His grace, undeniable.
His essence, unforgettable.

Sharing the wisdom of the ages, an
intergenerational sage he was.

Fond recollection of past conversation, means he's still here!
His wisdom still exists.
The pride still persists.
His light shines intense.
The man, in all his excellence and elegance – indeed, HE LIVED!

## 35

## THE ONE

In looking at you I thought you were the one
The one I see before me looks like you
But you are not that one

The things that come from your lips
The words that pierce my ears
The thoughts that you profess could not come from the one
Either you are not the one or you possess skills would rival
Thespis

You have evolved into a creature
You have become a dark legion of pain
You have brought back memories of the past pain, even when I
knew you not

Where are you from? The one who promised to love me.
Where did you go? The one who promised to support me.
Where are you? The one who promised to be happy for
me.

One time we grew together,
Now we grow apart.
I am happy that now I know


I am sad that I know now


You were everything to me for just that brief moment in time,

You were all that I needed
now you are the poison that kills me
You were the air I breathed
now you stifle me
You were the water I drank now you drown me.

I exist in flux, because of all the times you saved me from me
Now though painful – I must save me from you.

You are not the same and still I love you,
But I can't love you the way that you need to be loved and still
love myself.
I look keenly at you – but you are not THE ONE, THE ONE YOU
WERE.

## 36

# THE LESSONS OF LIFE

You taught the lessons of life . . .
we learned

We harnessed your energy and greatness
and became more than our wildest dreams
All because of you.

Hazel Williams- Ross

Your healing touch when ill, delivered comfort,
Your wise words when distraught, brought solace
Your hard work when we couldn't go on, brought safety
And you taught these lessons of life

I cannot remember when I met you first
because you were always there

Always there for me
Never just leave me be
Learning and teaching and lighting a fire in me
We learned, we yearned, we became because of you!

The greatest mystery of all revealed itself to you.
You embraced the unknown and I wanted to go too
You said it was not time, this lesson now was yours not mine

and with a breath and a smile you taught your final lesson on this plane

The time has been short and the pain hurts deep
The selfishness in me wants to hold you as you sleep
I wanted to learn more and achieve more and be more because of you.
Your life lessons teach me.
Your life lessons prepared me.

Thank God for you my Angel and your Lessons of Life.

## 37

# THE HUMMINGBIRD

*a dirge for Mr. Natural*

The hummingbird spoke gently to the high priest
letting him know, the time was coming.

The priest was special in that he would use nature to create
healing though food.

Drinking sweet nectar, the hummingbird
consumed the secrets of a life it had yet to behold. . . yet it knew.
There were signs and omens in the space of being
and the priest could see them all.

From the vantage of ascension, he started the journey
of knowing and growing and evolving into the ancestral ether.

While, *they* were scared and afraid and worried, *he* knew it would
be fine
. . . in time . . . Because the hummingbird said so.

Holding the messages of love and connection . . .
the priest prepared and the bird.......hummed

From temporal to spiritual the hummingbird transformed
into an inter-dimensional connection to *there*.

The priest did his part on the journey helping to prepare others on
their way.
"Don't cry for me. See the journey, let me be free", he said
The Hummingbird said it would be okay.

He did his preaching and his sharing and his loving until he
heard the call . . .
Then with a breath and a nod . . . he embraced the pall.

He ascended the throne that the hummingbird
said would be there . . . waiting . . . for him

His work *there* was finally done.
The other work had just begun.
His loved ones presented what was left to Olokun.
She received him warmly and HE soared!

All was okay. All was well.

Just like the Hummingbird said.

## 38

## YOU MADE ME FREE

I traveled near and far,
Over the sea and the land
I looked from the air and soared with the eagle
I probed the universe with my mind
Knowing that just beyond reach, you were there – but I could not find you

And then – as if a mirage – you appeared, strikingly wonderful
And I was set free.
You made me free,
Free to experience my love in ways that I thought were never possible
You took all that and made it plausible.

The freedom that I experienced was like that of a bird that made its first flight
I soared to heights that were anointed impossible – all
because of you; the wind beneath my wings

To some you were faceless
I kept you nameless
Together we were harmless until it came to the passion of love

You made me FREE!
Others couldn't understand that our freedom had no bounds – it
was a love story based on a myth
A tale that strangely began and will never end,

For our freedom was spiritually yoked
We were bound
Although our lovemaking existed only in my mind – I explored

I yearned to take my time in ensuring that each
new spot that I discovered was properly treated
I took care in scooping knowledge from your well of possibilities
and you,
You worshiped me as your king – it was supreme

Supreme freedom
From just a conversation –

It was instant relaxation,

Late nights and your voice
Put me on course and because of you I was free

Really, your physical time in my life was short but forget you –
I cannot
Remember you – Always I will Cherish
you – like a precious jewel
Now I know-

... THE FREEDOM OF LOVE!
YOU MADE ME FREE!

## STILL

The Sun rose still, as always it does

Clouds covered the light, yet hope peeked through the spaces

Reminding us that over there, up there, out there -- the radiant
light remains

Life like the light -- though dimmed -- does not end with a
chapter finished

But is invisibly written in volumes that will never be read on
this side

The sun sets still as always it does and the moon took her place
in the night sky. . .

A scant reminder that even in darkness,

The light is there . . . Shining.

Still.

## THE REIGN

I sit and wonder
Hearing sounds of thunder move beyond Sshhh,
Hush
Listen intently in the distance – Raindrops
falling, tinkling
Soft and sweet,
Like Lena's voice on satin sheets
The booming Thunder you thought you heard
Were really the notes from the Duke's verve
Summer, Winter, Spring or Fall
Cotton always high
When the storms of the classics come a' reigning by
Sweat of the brow,
Run down Music
of the reign Drown
my sorrow.
Now, I see my way . . .

## DADDY

*for Al Washington*
*(after watching Tim Burton's Big Fish)*

Daddy, you was an enigma
wrapped in a riddle at the crux of a lie
So for you I cry.

You were my should and my couldn't, my never would be and all
that I was
Looking toward you for the answers,
The truth came wrapped in gold upon a bed of silk
Societal expectation had retrained my mind to seek much less.
I love that which I knew and longed for that which I knew not

You was my baba.
Your lessons began in a story and ended in the truth
A truth that I was often too young to understand,
and even now I find myself pondering your words for revelation

There was some of me in you and some of you in me,
I ran from the me that I was destined to be.

Without reservation . . . I loved you still
Those who you love, I loved too not knowing why.

The secrets that you held close were the mysteries of
your untold generosity and the extent of your unconditional
love.

I loved you for being with me
I hated your for leaving me way too soon.

You were way too young
And though not here, you watch me still

Your stories make me laugh, still –
You live, *still* – within me, through your stories, by your tales.

*My Daddy,*
*My Angel –*
*MY TRUTH!*

## 42

# LONELY WOMAN

*(for Phyllis and those who are lonely)*

A lonely woman, not ready for a man
Frankly not ready for anything
But where she sits many long to stand
Her face - beautiful
Her posture - impeccable
Her hair - kinky like pre-sheared lamb's wool
The curves of her body would rival that of Isis
The strength of 10 amazons
And the compassion of a Southern Mammy
Yet she was a - lonely woman
Trying to protect her heart.

LONELY WOMAN

No one took the time to see what she was going though
No one really knew, I mean no one really knew
That inside she was crying and dying a thousand times
Deaths from the way that brothers treated her
You see she was a lady 'cause she chose to be
No one really know her pain for her virtues were amazing

If only I had known that she was lonely

LONELY WOMAN

In the beginning she was the belle of the ball
Like a Royal Princess going from person to person
spreading her joy
Like a honey-bee pollinating nature's garden, she was
Her beauty was legendary but to her mother's instructions
she was contrary when she saw him.
He was just like her mother described,
just like her father warned
Still he was what she wanted

Her heart skipped a beat and she thought this would make
her complete
In an instant, she imagined love with him – she
imagined his love not like others . . . he was
she imagined his compassion - not like others . . . it
was IT WAS!
He was her soulmate - or so she thought
No Longer Lonely

LONELY WOMAN

So, it happened - they were together
She and he, making music and
melody
It was all she'd hoped it'd be
He touched places inside of her that she never knew existed
She wanted more
Walking with her man she felt like a queen as subjects stopped to
gaze
She knew this was only a precursor to the night

Dark space, a place where her beauty reigned supreme
A place where she could be the freak, she needed to be
head, under toe, over elbow, behind back
Like that.
Deep into the annals of ecstasy almost piercing her lonely soul
No matter what was done, she knew he was the one Something
was missing
Can't quite place it - still lonely

## LONELY WOMAN

She had invited him into her temple
There to love and cherish her - like she knew he could
In her mind he was her God and she his Goddess
Nightly they sacrificed to each other with offerings and tributes
and promises of the future
The time progressed
The love digressed
There was distress
There would be thieves in the temple this night
Beautiful sister out in the jungle, making her way to provide But
the entire time she's thinking about the offering she'll make
tonight
Powerful thoughts invade her mind, making her pursue her
journey before the appointed
time - making her rise
So she left that place for her sacred space
Enter the temple she did
Into the anti-chamber she went
Preparing to take a trip on high
But there on the alter where she had made so many offerings lay
another
She was worshiping her
God In her temple

On her night LONELY

WOMAN

She was calm,
Poised even.
Never one to be caught out of style still a lady
Ahem-
She made herself known and the ritual ended quickly.
You have defiled my temple
You have degraded its sanctity
You have taken my love
Leave
Here
Now
He and she they left to flee
Leaving the Lonely Woman there to be ----- alone
This was as it was before
Not the same way but .... the same
With Sage she smudged
Candles she burned
Trying to erase the pain
It was too much to bear.

She reached for the apothecary's cure
Ready to leave this place
Ready to move from this space

A supernumerary few was all it took,
And it was no longer . . . she was no longer -- lonely.

If only I Had Known ....

# ~ 43 ~

## INDEED, I AM CRYING

Just for a moment there was a tear on my cheek.
I had no idea why. . .
Indeed, I was crying.

Crying for unintended consequence and the time to
recompense.
Indeed, I was crying . . .

Iyanlya said, "a good cry with a purpose was all I needed".
Instead of an agenda – I just needed my space.

I needed to release the pain of pleasure
and feel the lack of knowledge that made me into the man that I
was.

Searching and never finding.
Feeling and never knowing.
Being and never embracing.
Indeed, at this moment I was crying.

In the depth of my thought,
I could see the place to heal my soul

and plug the gushing well.

Yet seeing and obtaining are two different things.

I cry, because you hurt.
I cry, because I love.
I cry, because we are destined to try . . .

Just for a moment there was a tear on my cheek, and I had no idea
why . . .
Indeed, I was crying.

## ~ 44 ~

## I MISS YOU.

I miss the way you hold me with your voice and touch me with
your energy.
You accept me flawed and imperfect and wallowing in the
perfection of *me*.
I miss the way you caress my cares and push aside my fears in
just a moment.
You allow me to be strong and vulnerable without ever losing the
essence of my soul.
How can I miss you when I've truly never met you?
You like a distant memory, presently in front of me.
I pour libation to the possibility of our connection in realms of
undiscovered passion
I inhale deep and embrace the jasmine of your essence
Spicy and sweet and alluring and unique

But I've never touched you
Never inhaled you
Never seen you
Never experienced you...
How can it be that I miss one who I don't even know exists?
Yet I miss ...you.

## 45

## WHITE BIRD

White bird, write word.
Right moment, I learned.
Holding in my hands was a slice of life
The sound of light . . .
. . . that predated my existence.


I could feel the smooth purposeful heartbeat of the dove.

Her mission, to give physical rise to a soul that had already
journeyed to the realm beyond . . .

The work was done but *we* needed to see more.
The purity of unblemished essential love was there.
The pride of a fearless life well-lived,
The hurt of broken promises and lost loves,
The tenacity to lay a foundation for the one to come,

The pain of illness,
The freedom of surrender was
l there in the white bird.

The moment was predestined.
Clotho, Lachesis and Atropos looked on.
They felt the pain of the boy as real as it felt when they made the tapestry.
They knew --The loom never lied.
The sisters smiled slightly for the heart never dies --
When the love is true!

The boy wondered.
The bird waited.
The people gathered . . .
And at the moment where Chronos and Kairos found synergy --
There was release.

The white bird flew.
The people they knew
And at that moment *it* happened.
The bird flew to infinity
The love increased exponentially

And the end became a beginning!

## 46

## STILLNESS - A HAIKU

Thoughts gone off deep end
To take my life would be sin
There ends pain within

終わり

Award-winning actor, host, and author, **Rahman Johnson** has worked in TV, stage, and film for more than 25 years. He is Professor of Journalism and Communications at Edward Waters College, where he is the 2021 Professor of the Year.

Rahman was the host and producer of the television game show SPLAT, on Nickelodeon. His passion for creating a better sustainable community led him to serve in elected and appointed positions on the local, state, and federal levels. In every city he's lived, Rahman loves to give back through service in all of his work.

Johnson's stage and film credits, include the HBO original picture "First Time Felon" and the ABC Fantasy series "Sheena", Once on this Island and August Wilson's Radio Golf. He is committed to ensuring that the arts are an integral part of public-school education. He has appeared in media worldwide receiving many awards, including a Telly® Award, the Reginald Brack Award, and was named Achiever of the Century by the Thurgood Marshall Honors Society.

He is a member of the Society of Professional Journalists, Kappa Alpha Psi Fraternity, Inc., SAG/AFTRA, The Urban League, and the National Association of Black Journalists.

Today he hosts *The Rahman Experience* podcast and spreads a message of self-actualization and cultural-understanding though performing and lecturing around the world.

## www.rahmanjohnson.com

## @rahmanj

## www.facebook.com/rahmanjfans

CPSIA information can be obtained
at www.ICGtesting.com
Printed in the USA
JSHW030237071122
32718JS00001B/1